Finding Work You Love, When You Don't
Know Which Way to Go

Finding Work You Love, When You Don't Know Which Way to Go

A guide for twentysomethings

By

Stephanie K. Smith

ⴿ

Aventine Press

Stephanie Smith is available for speaking engagements and career coaching. You may contact her at ssmith@findingworkyoulove.com.

Published by Aventine Press
1023 4th Ave #204
San Diego, CA 92101
www.aventinepress.com

ISBN: 1-59330-253-3
Printed in the United States of America

Dedication

To my husband...my rock, who helped me find my way when I was lost.

To my parents, who provided the foundation upon which to build.

To those who are searching, may this book help you find your way.

Table of Contents

Introduction

How can you find work that makes you impatient to get out of bed in the morning when you do not even know what you really want to do?

Very early in my career, work had become a four-letter word for me. I became very discouraged and depressed over the thought of feeling this way for the rest of my working life. I became one of "the lost" in search of a better way to make a living. Five years of research and four career changes eventually culminated in the book you are now reading. I needed a book like this at the beginning of my career search, but at that point, no such book existed in a practical, concise, and action-oriented format.

Work can become fully integrated into your life; it no longer has to be something that you just tolerate until the end of the day and endure until the next weekend. After reading this book and working through the exercises, you will be able to describe your personality needs and use that information to analyze and create career options for lifelong enjoyment of your work experiences. You will learn to see your working life in a new way.

Contrary to what many believe, work can be enjoyable and even personally fulfilling. When you do fulfill your unique calling, work becomes more than a way to earn a living; it also fulfills the needs of your personality. When work is more than a paycheck, it becomes a source of joy.

PART I
The Promise Betrayed

Hold fast to dreams, for if dreams die, life is a broken winged bird that cannot fly. -Langston Hughes

What do you want to be when you grow up?

As a child, you were probably asked this countless times. At that time, there were as many different answers – a ballet dancer, a teacher, a fireman, a movie star, a doctor, a racecar driver – as there were people asking the question. Later, when you asked yourself that question – when choosing a school, a college major, or looking for a job – a queasy feeling hit you because you no longer had an answer. Work became something to endure – just one of those necessary parts of life that you neither look forward to nor enjoy, like paying taxes or getting a root canal. However, if you learn to plan your working life like you plan a vacation, a wedding, or some other enjoyable part of life, you will find that you can achieve more satisfying results and that you can actually enjoy the work you do for a living.

How can you expect to understand yourself and discover your useful, enjoyable place in this world when very seldom does anyone or anything help you discover your own uniqueness?

Enrolling in college right after high school has become a reality for many young people. Quite often attending college delays the time when young people become truly independent and resolve their identity issues. When one stage of personal development has not been resolved, a person cannot move on to the next stage. If an individual cannot make deliberate decisions and choices, especially about a career, some level of confusion may result. Consequentially, scores of twentysomethings and even thirtysomethings drift aimlessly from one job to another.

After I graduated from college and started working full-time, I felt an emptiness inside me. I felt lost, stuck, and unsure about what to do. Perhaps you feel that way too. Work was unfulfilling for me, and I felt I had no real reason to get up each morning, other than to pay the bills. Over time, I found out that I felt stuck because I *was* stuck. I was stuck with an unresolved identity crisis. I needed to go back and make a conscious effort to find my true identity and then match that identity with work I could love.

CHAPTER 1
The Quarterlife Crisis

It was supposed to be simple. Go to school, graduate, get a good job, have a family, and live happily ever after. Right?

As a student, you had benchmarks to measure your progress. You received grades and report cards. You knew what was expected and what you had to do to succeed. In the "real world", the rules are not so clear, but somehow you were magically supposed to know which career you would excel at and enjoy. What happens if you do not know which career to choose? You try and try again, and settle for a less-than-enjoyable career.

In school, you are not often taught to look within as a means of finding your path in life. Rather, you are taught to memorize the words of others. When you do well in an academic subject, you think you should pursue a career in that area. Sometimes that works, but more often it does not. You can shorten the process of finding your path and achieve better results if you begin by knowing the personality traits that make you unique and then use that knowledge to find equally unique work experiences.

These feelings of being "lost" and "stuck" are actually fairly widespread for people in their twenties. Unfortunately, many twentysomethings do not realize that this is such a common experience. A debt of gratitude goes to Alexandra Robbins and Abby Wilner for speaking so openly and publicly about the "quarterlife crisis" (Robbins, 7) in their book *Quarterlife Crisis: the Unique Challenges of Life in Your Twenties.* While Robbins and Wilner describe the challenges of entering the real world after college, I propose that there is a larger pattern at work. It is not only the twentysomethings just leaving college who experience difficulty finding meaningful work; I contend that all twentysomethings experience that difficulty if they have not resolved the earlier developmental stage of identity that begins and is ideally resolved during adolescence.

Robbins and Wilner state in *Quarterlife Crisis* that the "quarterlife crisis" (Robbins, 7) is an identity crisis[1]. After some time in the real world, twentysomethings often question whether this is all there is to life: eat, sleep, go to work, and hate your job. Is this all life has to offer? A real sense of disappointment sets in. For recent college graduates, there is a profound realization that higher education has not prepared them for the decisions they have to make. They are trying to discover the meaning of life and find fulfillment. They want to love what they do, and to derive satisfaction and happiness from it. They may change jobs often, move to a new city, but the feeling that they should be doing more and should be more fulfilled with their work does not go away.

Who are you?

That can seem like an unfair question – overly simplistic while at the same time difficult to answer. It does not have to be such a difficult question. However, if you have traveled through our current education system, public or private, you could probably recite more about who our first presidents were, who the first men on the moon were, who led the March on Washington, and who broke the color line in national baseball more than you could answer the question, "Who are *you*?" Most people try to answer that question by stating what they do for a living. "I am a teacher, I am a programmer, I am a consultant." But what happens if you lose your job or do not know what kind of career you want to pursue? Are you nobody? It can feel that way, because the search for identity has not been resolved.

The following excerpt from *Quarterlife Crisis* illustrates what can happen if you do not go back and address the issue of identity. One of the twentysomethings interviewed for *Quarterlife Crisis* responded that her father had given her the following advice:

> Look at me, I am 58 years old and I still have not yet found an ideal job that I absolutely love through and through. So I try different things until I find something that I am good at and enjoy. But there is something out there exactly for you, and until you run into that perfect fit, you try out several different venues and figure out what you don't like.[2]

This is the trial-and-error method of finding out who you are, and it is not terribly efficient. Instead, you could take some time to research your own personality and use that information to create career satisfaction and fulfillment now.

Life in your twenties can be full of opportunity, as well as great confusion. Beginning life on your own, with your own place, your own bills, and your own job, can weigh heavily on twentysomethings. This, combined with not fully understanding yourself, can make it a period of crisis. I experienced such a crisis myself and propose that some level of crisis is quite universal for today's twentysomethings.

The theories of psychological development assert that there are several stages through which one passes: infancy to childhood, adolescence to young adulthood, middle adulthood to maturity. Each stage has a period of crisis that must be resolved before one can freely move onto the next stage. Herein lies the difficulty for twentysomethings. According to psychosocial development theory, the stage that deals with identity issues should be resolved in the teen years. During this stage, you work to achieve a sense of identity in a number of areas, including occupation. However, quite often this stage is not fully resolved between the ages of 12 and 18.

Taking the time to resolve the developmental stage of identity, regardless of your age now, will allow you to move on in your life and to answer the questions that led you to this book in the first place: Who am I? What am I going to do with my life?

CHAPTER 2
Being Lost

What am I going to do with my life?

I asked myself this question many times, and heard it asked by well-meaning adults all too often. As a high school student, I thought I was doing everything "right". Somehow I thought that if I did all the right things, I would achieve the right results, even if I did not have a clue what to expect.

In high school I joined everything: I was in the art club, the school play, on the student council. I played volleyball, ran fundraisers, lobbied for school improvements, made honor roll every quarter, received academic awards and scholarships, joined honor societies, and graduated as class valedictorian. I succeeded at everything I tried and felt I was doing everything I was supposed to do. I was always told to do well in school, become a well-rounded person, and go to a good college. Although it was never stated, I always assumed that if I did all those things my parents, teachers, and other adults in my life told me to do, I would become a happy and successful person. After all, it worked for them, right?

In college, I did more of the same. I earned all As, made the dean's list, joined a few academic clubs, checked out the student government association, tried out for a play, took self-defense classes, and made new friends. I entered college undecided about a major; when it was time to select one, I chose the area that had interested me the most in high school and college up to that point, history. Four years after entering college, I graduated *summa cum laude* with a dual degree in History and Education, a teaching certificate, and a job teaching middle school for the next school year. At graduation, I felt once again that I had done everything I was supposed to do. I had done everything right and was about to reap my rewards. All that was left was to await the right results. I would be happy and successful. I would reach the students in my classes, make a difference, be respected, and have a meaningful career.

Reality was not quite that simple. I soon discovered that I did not enjoy teaching seventh grade social studies. The curriculum was too advanced for the twelve and thirteen year olds I taught, many of whom read on a third grade level. As a brand new teacher, I naturally had to cope with serious behavior problems in my classes. Students talked out of turn, were disrespectful to each other and to me, and fought with each other physically in my classroom.

During that first year, I was laughed at, and talked about; my principal rated me an unsatisfactory teacher for the first four months I taught school. I cried every morning before going to work, had no appetite, lost weight, and became depressed. I did not see a way out of the situation. I did not feel I had anything else to offer the world. I had prepared to be a teacher and now I was failing at it and hating every minute I was there. Had I gone to college to break up fights between children? Weekends were not long enough and no length of spring or summer break made up for the fact that I hated what I did Monday to Friday from September to June. I was angry at myself for not figuring this out sooner, but I was even angrier at the parents, older relatives, teachers and other authority figures in my life who had never told me that work would be like this. Despite my anger, I said nothing because I was ashamed that I was having such a hard time adjusting, and I believed that I must be the only young person who felt this way. This was *not* the reward I had expected after all that hard work I did when I was in school.

Miraculously, I made it through my first year of teaching and the introduction into the ubiquitous "real world". Not knowing what else to do for income, I signed up for another year of teaching. Everyone I spoke to had convinced me that if I made it through the first year, the second year would be a great improvement. With that, I thought I owed it to myself to try another year. So September came again and there I was, facing another year of doing something I hated. I often found myself thinking that I would not mind teaching so much – as long as there were no students. So what was I really doing? I did not like my job, nor the person I was becoming. Most of the day, I was yelling at students in order to be heard over their noise, which I was supposed to control. Although I did not yell as much in my second year as I did in my first, I felt I was acting as a warden. I had to keep a firm watch over the masses so they did not erupt into chaos. I decided I did not want to teach anymore.

But what else was I supposed to do? My college sweetheart, now my husband, kept reassuring me that I could do anything I put my mind to doing. I was smart, personable, and a quick learner. I worked hard and got along well with others. What employer would not want someone like that on staff? Then he would follow up with the question that would send me into a tailspin, "What do you want to do?" I had no answer for this question. Strangely enough, I had not given much thought to what I really wanted to do. At that moment, I simply wanted to be independently wealthy so that I did not have to work anymore. Then he would ask me, "What would you do with your time if you did not work?" My answer was very cliché: "whatever I wanted to do." Of course, that was not an answer; I did not have an answer and that was the problem.

Where do you go for advice? What action do you take to find out what you want to do? I did not want to prepare for another career again only to find out later that it was something I did not want to do either. I kept thinking that there had to be a better way. I decided to return to school for a master's degree. What else was I going to do? I felt unprepared to do anything else. I decided to get a master's degree in history, the same area as my undergraduate major. Then I started wondering what was I going to do with a master's degree in history once I completed it. I had no idea, but I imagined that I would figure something out. I applied to my alma mater, was accepted into their master's program, and even received a small fellowship. I did not know how my husband and I would pay our expenses, given my taking a $25,000 pay cut to go back to school full-time, and without any real goal in mind. One month before the program was to begin, I withdrew.

More uncertain than ever, but at least glad I did not take on the expense of school just to find myself back in the same situation again, I fell into a depression for the next several months. I began going to counseling and it was there that I first realized I was angry at the way the "real world" was turning out and felt deceived by all the well-meaning adults in my life. Why did no one tell me it was going to be this difficult? Why did no one tell me work would be horrible? Why didn't I know what I wanted to do with my life? At the time, I had no answers.

Still stumbling, I decided to return to the only work I knew I could do – teaching. I signed up to become a substitute teacher in the same district where I had been a full-time teacher. Since I only earned $50 a day as a substitute, I also began tutoring at an after school learning center. I still hated the classroom part of substitute teaching and felt awful about being a substitute when I used to have my own classroom. I would ask myself, how did such a supposedly "smart" person come to this? I was angry and still depressed.

I decided to look for a full-time teaching position and took a long-term substitute position in a sixth grade social studies class. In a few weeks, I was offered the position on a permanent basis. I had essentially made a complete circle, and I was really no better for it. I still hated going to work everyday, and now I was depressed on top of everything else. The students were no easier to control – in fact, they were worse. It was late October and they had already caused their first teacher to quit. I returned to counseling, cried a lot, and felt like a failure. I felt miserable about myself and about life in general. I looked forward to nothing. The day I went to the assistant principal to hand in my resignation, she asked me that same haunting question that I had been grappling with since I graduated from college, "What are going to do with the rest of your life?" I still did not have an answer.

I scoured the newspapers and websites for job listings and sent my resume to anyone or any place that looked remotely promising. I took a job temping as a receptionist for all of two days before I realized I felt even more horrible answering phones and making photocopies for $9 an hour. I knew I could do much more.

I then found an ad in the paper for tour guides in Washington, D.C. It sounded like fun, they were willing to train me, and so I gave it a shot. That "shot" lasted for two years. I learned to drive a tour bus, earned a commercial driver's license, and began giving tours of our nation's capital. I enjoyed the work for a while, but soon the familiar feelings that I was not living up to my potential returned with a vengeance. I began reading, researching, and trying to find out who I was and what I wanted to do in this life. I felt I had to have a purpose, a reason for being here. I figured we could not have been put on this earth to muddle through life hating 70% of our existence and just living for retirement, could we?

Over years of searching, I began to learn what made me tick, why I enjoyed the things I did, and how I could relate that knowledge to choosing what work I would enjoy. I now have learned to incorporate work experiences and my other interests into my life so that they will fulfill me and bring me satisfaction. Figuring out what made me tick led me to the field of project management, to completing an MBA, to writing this book, and to teaching others how to find work they enjoy.

I do not have all of life figured out, but I look forward to each new day – whether it is a workday or weekend. I understand who I am and what I enjoy. Like many other people, I found my way to this awareness after much struggle. Through my negative work experiences, I found out what I did *not* want to do. In the process, I discovered a better way. The chapters of this book encapsulate what I learned through five years of research, incessant reading, and plain old trial and error.

PART II

The Keys to Finding Work You Love

Do not follow where the path may lead. Go instead where there is no path and leave a trail. - Ralph Waldo Emerson

Understanding your personality is like having the secret decoder to your own happiness. You will begin to understand not only what you like, but also why you like it. Understanding your personality gives you power over your own happiness.

CHAPTER 3
Your Personality

Personality can be defined as the stable set of individual characteristics that make you unique[3]; it is a constant set of thoughts, feelings, motivations, and behaviors that are expressed in different circumstances. Stability is important to this definition because even though your interests may change over time, your personality will not. Even in childhood, your personality provides valuable clues to what your adult personality will be like. Your personality is a collection of traits you were born with and experiences you have had. However, at its core, your personality has been constant since you were a child. The way you express your personality has changed, but your personality itself has not.

Personality is made up of characteristics that explain why you do what you do. Understanding your own personality will provide valuable insight into why you like certain aspects of your work and not others. It will also help you discover the type of work that would provide you with enjoyment and fulfillment. Matching your personality to your purpose can bring great joy, satisfaction, fulfillment, and a path out of the "quarterlife crisis" (Robbins, 7).

If you are movie buff, you might recall what Agent Smith said in the movie *The Matrix Reloaded*: "It is purpose that created us, it is purpose that connects us, it is purpose that pulls us, it is purpose that guides us, drives us, defines us, and binds us."[4] By discovering your purpose, you will find a major key to self-fulfillment. It is good to know that you like to do something, for instance, to work with children, to be around art, to write. However, it is even better to understand why you like to do something, because that understanding gives you the insight to realize your purpose: "It is with the why that you have power".[5]

Getting Technical – Erikson's Stages of Development

Erik Erickson (1902 – 1994) is considered the father of psychosocial development. He outlined an influential theory of human development, and his theories can provide insight for answering the key question, "Who am I?"

Erickson proposes that there are eight stages of development in a person's life. Four occur during childhood, three occur in adulthood, and one occurs as we pass from childhood into adulthood. This last stage between childhood and adulthood is the identity stage, and is of great interest to those looking to answer the question "Who am I?"

Each of Erickson's developmental stages depends on the one before, and each is marked by a conflict or a crisis. A crisis is a crucial point or situation that often serves as a turning point. It can also be an emotionally stressful event or traumatic change in your life. When the environment makes demands on people, conflicts arise. You make progress and grow by successfully navigating a developmental stage and solving its key crisis. You stagnate and become weaker when a crisis is not successfully resolved. Only when each conflict is resolved does the person have enough strength to deal with the next stage of development.[6]

The following is a description of five of Erikson's eight development stages, ending with the identity stage. (There are three additional developmental stages that follow the identity stage, but they will not be covered here.) For additional information about Erikson's theory of development and descriptions of all eight stages, consult *Tools and Resources* in Part 5.

Stage 1: Trust vs. Mistrust

During an infant's first year of life, she learns to trust her mother, father, or other primary caretakers. If the caretaker is responsive to the infant, she learns to trust. She will eventually use this lesson in later stages as she develops loving and working relationships as well as the lifelong expectation that the world will be a pleasant place to live. Should the child be neglected during this stage, she learns mistrust and will have difficulty in later stages developing trusting relationships.[7]

Stage 2: Autonomy vs. Shame

During a child's first three years of life, the crucial lesson of using the toilet is learned. During this time, he is working through the stage of autonomy (self rule) versus shame. Learning the control of bodily functions later translates into a sense of independence that the child can control his own actions. If a child is punished too harshly or restrained too much during this stage, he could learn to doubt himself and this would cause greater difficulties in later stages.[8]

Stage 3: Initiative vs. Guilt

By the time a child starts pre-school and kindergarten, ages four and five, play has become a valuable means of learning. Children make up games, imaginary friends, play "make believe", and discover new ways to play old games. Successfully completing this stage allows a child to further the lesson of independence by reinforcing her confidence in taking initiative. However, the child that is crippled from the fear of doing something wrong will experience guilt and self-doubt that will continue to hinder her in later stages.[9]

Stage 4: Industry vs. Inferiority

In this stage a child, age six through eleven, finds that work in the form of schoolwork becomes very important. There is a shift from play to a desire for achievement and completion. Children who find success in school and other related activities further develop the feeling of independence and competency. Children who find school difficult may develop feelings of inferiority and inadequacy that will carry over into later stages in life, such as on the job and in relationships unless the stage is revisited.[10]

Stage 5: Identity vs. Identity Confusion

According to Erickson, it is during adolescence that children begin to seek their true identity and a sense of self that is separate from their parents. The central question of this stage is one many are still asking today, "Who am I?"[11] This stage begins in puberty and continues until roughly the age of 18 or 20.

In developing an identity, a person must integrate the healthy resolution of all earlier conflicts, take all that has been learned about life and self and mold it into a unified self-image that is meaningful within the community.[12] This is in fact an "Identity Crisis". Erikson considered this the single most significant conflict a person must face. In addition to this identity crisis, this is also a time to transition from childhood into adulthood. No wonder this stage is so difficult and takes many well into their twenties and sometimes beyond to resolve. When this stage is successfully negotiated, a person finds a place to make useful contributions in the community.

This is a brief synopsis of the first five of Erickson's eight stages of development. If you would like more information on Erickson's theory of development, please consult Part 5 for *Tools and Resources*.

Given Erikson's theories and today's reality, how can you realistically be expected to figure out who you are by the time you are 18? When you consider the fact that teenagers who attend college right after high school will not begin their careers until after college or graduate school, that already puts them in their early to mid-twenties before actually entering the work force. At that point, the discovery that you do not like your chosen career comes as quite a shock and disappointment. In addition, the economy has been doing nosedives in many industries, and many young people find that the jobs they were educated to do are no longer available. It is no wonder that twentysomethings wind up feeling confused, lied to, betrayed, and angry.

Many young people have been returning home to live with their parents as they save money, search for a job, or try to figure themselves out. According to an online survey of 1,108 students by MonsterTrak, a job Web site for college students, about sixty-four percent of the 2004 college graduating class polled planned to move home after graduation, and thirty-eight percent expected to stay at home for more than seven months.[13] Even Erikson stated, "As technological advances put more and more time between early school life and the young person's final access to specialized work, the stage of adolescing becomes an even more marked and conscious period".[14] So in essence, the stage at which the identity crisis is resolved has become delayed. Therefore, one's twenties becomes the perfect time to do the work to discover your personality and identity.

Going Deeper – Jung's Theory of Personality

Carl Jung (1875 – 1961) made the exploration of "inner space" his life's work. He believed that the goal of life is to realize the true self.[15] Not only can Jung's theory of personality assist in answering the "Who am I?" question, but also the "What should I be doing with my life?" question. Jung developed a theory of personality that begins with understanding the difference between introversion and extroversion. Introverts are people who prefer their internal world of thoughts, feelings, and dreams. Extroverts prefer the external world of things, people, and activities. Neither extroversion nor introversion is better or worse than the other, and everyone has a natural tendency toward one or the other. While an introvert can behave as an extrovert, it requires extra effort. Likewise, an extrovert can behave as an introvert, but that too would require extra effort and energy.[16]

Both introverts and extroverts need to deal with the inner and outer world. There is no way of getting around that. Each has a preferred way of dealing with the world, one where each is comfortable and excels. Jung suggests that there are four basic ways of dealing with the world. These ways are called functions.[17]

1. The first function is sensing – getting information through the senses. A sensing person is good at looking, listening, and understanding the world through perception.

2. The second function is thinking – evaluating information or ideas logically rather than just an intake of information.

3. The third function is intuiting – a kind of perception that works outside the usual processes. Intuition is based on perception, but emerges out of the integration of large amounts of information, rather than just from the senses.

4. The fourth function is feeling. Feeling, like thinking, evaluates information, but through feeling one weighs one's overall emotional response to the information.

Everyone has all four of these functions to varying degrees. The best developed of the four is the superior function and is the overall preference when dealing with the world. The secondary function supports the superior function. The tertiary function is slightly less developed and the inferior function is very poorly developed. Most people develop only one or two functions, but Jung believed that the goal in life should be to develop all four functions over the course of a lifetime.[18]

By revisiting Erikson's identity stage and Jung's theory of personality, you can shave years off your search for self and begin to discover work you will love now. Otherwise, how can you expect to discover who you really are if you never do the work to do just that. Trial-and-error can be a very long and painful road. It should be common practice for twentysomethings to revisit the stage of identity during college and graduate school, and certainly upon completion of their formal education and entry into the workforce.

CHAPTER 4
Where do I start?

Jung's theory of personality types and functions were so revealing of people's personalities that Katharine Briggs and her daughter Isabel Briggs Myers developed a paper-and-pencil test to help people determine their personality type. This test is now called the Myers-Briggs Type Indicator® (MBTI®). There are sixteen MBTI types that reveal a great deal about your personality such as your likes and dislikes, your likely career preferences, and your compatibility with others. The MBTI is not a judgmental assessment because each type has a blend of strengths and drawbacks that serve to make up a full range of personality. The MBTI can provide valuable insight into your personality and help you answer the question of "Who am I?" so that you can soon answer the question "What should I be doing?"

The Myers-Briggs Type Indicator® and the MBTI® are registered trademarks of Consulting Psychologists Press,

Inc. Additional information on the MBTI and taking the assessment can be found at their website, http://www.cpp.com/products/mbti/index.asp.

There are also wonderful free resources and assessments on the Internet for determining your personality type. You can find some of them in *Tools and Resources* in Part 5. I recommend that you now spend a little time taking a personality assessment and determine your four-letter personality type.

By reading through the descriptions of Jung's personality functions in the next four sections, you may begin to see yourself on one side or the other; this will help you discover your four-letter personality type. The descriptions in the following sections of the four-letter personality types described by Myers-Briggs are adapted from the quiz "What is Your Personality Type?" created by Barbara Barron-Tieger and Paul Tieger. The full version of this quiz can be found at http://www.personalitytype.com/quiz.asp. As you read these sections, try to think of yourself as you really are and are most comfortable, not as you wish you were, or have to be at work.

Extrovert or Introvert

The following is an overview of extroverts and introverts.

Extroverts (E):
- Have high energy

- Talk more than listen

- Think out loud

- Act, then think

- Like to be around people a lot

- Prefer a public role

- Can sometimes be easily distracted

- Prefer to do lots of things at once

- Are outgoing and enthusiastic

Introverts (I):

- Have quiet energy

- Listen more than talk

- Think quietly to themselves

- Think, then act

- Feel comfortable being alone

- Prefer to work "behind-the-scenes"

- Have good powers of concentration

- Prefer to focus on one thing at a time

- Are self-contained and reserved

Does one list describe you more than the other? If so, that one is most likely your preference. Write down your preference on the line provided and the one letter abbreviation in the parentheses.

My preference is 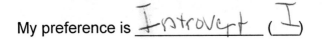 Introvert (I)

Sensing or Intuitive

The following is an overview of sensors and intuitives.

Sensors (S):

- Focus on details and specifics

- Admire practical solutions

- Notice details and remember facts

- Are pragmatic – see what is

- Live in the here-and-now

- Trust actual experience

- Like to use established skills

- Like step-by-step instructions

- Work at a steady pace

Intuitives (N):

- Focus on the big picture and possibilities

- Admire creative ideas

- Notice anything new or different

- Are inventive

- Think about future implications

- Trust their gut instincts

- Prefer to learn new skills

- Like to figure things out for themselves

- Work in bursts of energy

If one list describes you better than the other, then that one is most likely your personality preference. Write down your preference on the line provided and the one letter abbreviation in the parentheses.

My preference is _Intuitive_ (_N_)

Thinking or Feeling

The following is an overview of thinkers and feelers.

Thinkers (T):

- Make decisions objectively

- Appear cool and reserved

- Are most convinced by rational arguments

- Are honest and direct

- Value honesty and fairness

- Take few things personally

- Tend to see flaws

- Are motivated by achievement

- Argue or debate issues for fun

Feelers (F):

- Decide based on their values and feelings

- Appear warm and friendly

- Are most convinced by how they feel

- Are diplomatic and tactful

- Value harmony and compassion

- Take many things personally

- Are quick to compliment others

- Are motivated by appreciation

- Avoid arguments and conflict

The list that most closely describes you is most likely your personality preference. Write down your preference on the line provided and the one letter abbreviation in the parentheses.

My preference is ___Thinker___ (_T_)

Judging or Perceiving

The following is an overview of judgers and perceivers.

Judgers (J):

- Make most decisions pretty easily

- Are serious and conventional

- Pay attention to time and are prompt

- Prefer to finish projects

- Work first, play later

- Want things decided

- See the need for most rules

- Like to make and stick with plans

- Find comfort in schedules

Perceivers (P):

- May have difficulty making decisions

- Are playful and unconventional

- Are less aware of time and run late

- Prefer to start projects

- Play first, work later

- Want to keep their options open

- Question the need for many rules

- Like to keep plans flexible

- Want the freedom to be spontaneous

The list that most closely describes you is most likely your personality preference. Write down your preference on the line provided and the one letter abbreviation in the parentheses.

My preference is ___Perceiver___ (_P_)   *P? not sure*

Now write down the four-letter abbreviations in parentheses from each of the previous sections.

If you have not taken a personality assessment, please pause in your reading and confirm your four-letter personality code by taking one of the assessments mentioned in Part 5, *Tools and Resources*.

CHAPTER 5

What does my type say about me?

In the sections that follow you will find a synopsis of the 16 personality types, identified by four-letter codes, which are the basis of the Myers-Briggs assessment. The descriptions found here were adapted from "Current Topics in Psychology" by Dr. C. George Boeree at www.fenichel. com and from Barbara Barron-Tieger and Paul Tieger, authors of *Do What You Are* at http://www.personalitytype. com/quiz.asp.

You can find a wealth of information on your particular personality type on the Internet. There is so much information online that you can put your four-letter code into any search engine and receive dozens of hits. One of my favorites can be found at http://www.personalitypage. com/high-level.html. Others can be found listed in the *Tools and Resources* listed in Part 5.

ENFJ

Extroverted Intuitive Feeling Judging "The Givers" or "The Teacher"	
Energetic	Idealistic
Sociable	Charming
Influential	Warm
Sensitive	Caring
Tenacious	Popular
Leader	Charismatic

ENFJs tend to be friendly, outgoing, enthusiastic, affectionate, articulate, and tactful. They are very empathetic but can be easily hurt. They tend to be creative, original, decisive, passionately opinionated, productive, organized, and responsible. The most important thing to ENFJs is their relationships and the opportunity to communicate and connect with others.

ENFJs are easy speakers. They tend to idealize their friends, make good parents, but have a tendency to allow others to take advantage of them. They tend to make good therapists, teachers, executives, and salespeople.

ENFP

Extroverted Intuitive Feeling Perceptive "The Inspirers" or "The Champion"	
Charming	Charismatic
Warm	Ingenious
Sympathetic	Interactive
Communicative	Open minded
Imaginative	Gentle

ENFPs tend to be enthusiastic, talkative, outgoing, clever, curious, and playful. They are often deeply caring, sensitive, gentle, highly innovative, creative, optimistic, unique, and have a natural gift for inspiring others. They are adaptable and resourceful but sometimes disorganized. The most important thing to ENFPs is freedom to see possibilities, make connections, and be with a variety of people.

ENFPs love novelty and surprises. They are big on emotions and expression. They are susceptible to muscle tension and tend to be hyper-alert and feel self-conscious. They are good at sales, advertising, politics, and acting.

ENTJ

Extroverted Intuitive Thinking Judging "The Executives" or "The Field Marshals"	
Outgoing	Assertive
Decisive	Systematic
Analytical	Inspires others
Objective	Sees the "big picture"

ENTJs tend to be friendly, strong willed, and outspoken. They are honest, goal oriented, logical and demanding of themselves and others. As such, they are driven to demonstrate competence, are creative with a global perspective, and are decisive, organized, and efficient. The most important thing to ENTJs is demonstrating their competence and making important things happen.

ENTJs are often in charge at home. They like organization and structure and tend to make good executives and administrators.

ENTP

Extroverted Intuitive Thinking Perceptive "The Visionaries" or "The Inventors"	
Easygoing	Innovative
Enthusiastic	Motivating
Non-conforming	Inspirational
Instigator	Multi-talented
Optimistic	Likes to be challenged

ENTPs tend to be friendly, charming, and outgoing. They are quick-witted, energetic, ingenious, imaginative, and creative. Additionally, they are curious, flexible, logical, and analytical. ENTPs value creativity as well as new possibilities and challenges.

ENTPs are lively people. They are good at analysis and tend to make good entrepreneurs.

ESFJ

Extroverted Sensing Feeling Judging "The Caregivers" or "The Providers"	
Warm	Loyal
Traditional	Conservative
Dutiful	Nurturing
Practical	Sociable
Naturally talented at working with others	Organized

ESFJs tend to be active, friendly, and energetic. They are outgoing, affectionate, and talkative. Likewise, they are concerned about others and are careful to be polite and cooperative. They are realistic, literal, conscientious, highly sensitive, and easily hurt. They are also organized, responsible, and conventional. The most important thing to ESFJs is their relationships and helping people in real and practical ways.

ESFJs like harmony. They may be dependent, first on parents and later on spouses. They wear their hearts on their sleeves and tend to excel in service occupations involving personal contact.

ESFP

Extroverted Sensing Feeling Perceptive "The Performer" or "The Artisan"	
Outgoing	Unpredictable
Charming	Cheerful
Open-minded	Generous
Optimistic	Enjoys life
Fun to be with	Conversationalist

ESFPs tend to be warm, gregarious, and playful as well as impulsive, curious, and talkative. They are sensitive, caring, gentle, social, and unpredictable with a great zeal for life. They are active, responsive, and highly aware of the physical world. The most important thing to ESFPs is freedom to be spontaneous, have fun, and enjoy the company of others.

ESFPs are very generous and impulsive with a low tolerance for anxiety. They tend to make good performers, like public relations, and love the phone.

ESTJ

Extroverted Sensing Thinking Judging "The Guardians" or "The Supervisors"	
Outgoing	Faithful and responsible
Punctual	Practical
Takes charge	Conservative
Decisive	Traditional
Rational	Interested in getting the job done

ESTJs tend to be energetic, friendly, outspoken, productive, organized and efficient. They are realistic and sensible, but often skeptical about new or untested ideas. They are honest and direct to the point of bluntness, quick decision makers, opinionated, traditional, serious, and accountable. The most important thing to ESTJs is doing the right thing and being in charge.

ESTJs are responsible and loyal to the workplace. They are realistic, down-to-earth, orderly, and love tradition. They tend to excel at teaching, banking, political office, and management.

ESTP

Extroverted Sensing Thinking Perceptive "The Doers" or "The Promoters"	
Outgoing	Diplomatic
Action oriented	Witty and clever
Unpredictable	Generous
Observing	Socially sophisticated
Resourceful	Troubleshooter

ESTPs tend to be active, adventurous, impulsive, talkative, and curious. They are casual, adaptive, and free spirited. They also tend to be logical and calm but capable of great humor, fun, and charm. They are observant, present in the moment, literal, and practical. The most important thing to ESTPs is the freedom to have fun and to fully experience life in the here and now.

ESTPs are action-oriented people, often sophisticated, and sometimes ruthless. They tend to make good promoters and entrepreneurs.

INFJ

Introverted Intuitive Feeling Judging "The Protectors" or "The Counselors"	
Peace-loving	Intuitive
Articulate	Empathetic
Committed	Caring
Enjoys being of service to others	Quiet

INFJs tend to be creative, original, independent, thoughtful, warm, and sensitive. They are global thinkers with great passion for their unique vision. They are also cautious, deliberate, and like to plan. They are often organized, productive, decisive, reserved, and polite. INFJs are idealistic and faithful to their vision.

INFJs are serious students and workers who really want to contribute. They are private and easily hurt. They tend to make good therapists, general practitioners, and ministers.

INFP

Introverted Intuitive Feeling Perceptive "The Idealists" or "The Healers"	
Spiritual or Philosophical	Committed to people and causes
Perceptive	Capacity for deep caring
Likes harmony	Guided by strong inner sense of values

INFPs tend to be quiet, reserved, and kind. They are deeply passionate, sensitive, and easily hurt. They are also loving, dedicated to those close to them, creative, original, and imaginative. INFPs tend to be curious, flexible in small matters, and nonconforming. The most important thing to

INFPs is their deeply held beliefs and living in harmony with their values.

INFPs are idealistic, self-sacrificing, and somewhat cool or reserved. They are very family and home oriented, but do not relax well. They tend to work in the fields of psychology, architecture, and religion, but usually not in business.

INTJ

Introverted Intuitive Thinking Judging "The Scientists" or "The Masterminds"	
Has personal mission	Highly independent
Introspective	Decisive
Driven by inner ideas and possibilities	Concerned with organization

INTJs tend to be autonomous, aloof, and intellectual. They are imaginative, innovative, unique, critical, analytical, and logical. They can also be intellectually curious and are driven to learn and increase their competence and knowledge. INTJs tend to be socially cautious, reserved, organized, and definitive. The most important thing to INTJs is their independence and being able to live according to their own standards.

INTJs are the most independent of all types. They love logic and ideas, and they are drawn to scientific research.

INTP

Introverted Intuitive Thinking Perceptive "The Thinkers" or "The Architects"	
Impersonal	Reflective
Visionary	Reserved
Ability to concentrate	Analytical
Values ideas and abstract thinking	Intellectual

INTPs tend to be quiet, independent, private, logical, principled, and unemotional. They are creative, ingenious, innovative, global thinkers as well as curious and driven to increase their competence. They tend to be casual, adaptive, nonconforming and unpredictable. The most important thing to INTPs is their privacy and the opportunity to solve complex problems in unique ways.

INTPs are often described as faithful, preoccupied, and forgetful. They tend to be very precise in their use of language, are good at logic and math and tend to make good philosophers and theoretical scientists.

ISFJ

Introverted Sensing Feeling Judging "The Nurturers" or "The Protectors"	
Deeply compassionate	Sensitive
Faithful	Dependable
Conservative	Values a regulated life
Hard worker	Attends to details
Private	Unassuming
Self-sacrificing	Sometimes misunderstood

ISFJs tend to be cautious, gentle, thoughtful, and hesitant until they know people well then they are quite affectionate and caring. They are very literal and aware of the physical world. ISFJs are uncompromising about personal standards and are easily offended. They are diligent, conscientious, organized, and decisive. The most important thing to ISFJs is living a stable, predictable life and helping people in real ways.

ISFJs are service and work oriented. They may suffer from fatigue and tend to be attracted to troublemakers. They tend to be good nurses, teachers, general practitioners, librarians, and middle managers.

ISFP

Introverted Sensing Feeling Perceptive "The Artists" or "The Composers"	
Retiring	Reserved
Cheerful	Optimistic
Observant	Generous
Loyal helper	Receptive
Independent	Trusting

ISFPs tend to be kind, humble, highly empathetic, thoughtful, faithful, and affectionate with those they know well. They are sensitive to criticism and are easily hurt. They are quiet, soft-spoken, gentle, adaptable, responsive, curious, realistic, and down to earth. The most important thing to ISFPs is feeling peaceful and harmonious with the people and places that matter most to them.

ISFPs tend to be shy and retiring; they are not talkative, but like action. They tend to like the arts (painting, drawing, sculpting, composing, dancing) and nature.

ISTJ

Introverted Sensing Thinking Judging "The Duty Fulfillers" or "The Inspectors"	
Serious	Dependable
Loyal	Steadfast
Patient	Sensible
Conservative	Values honesty

ISTJs tend to be cautious, conservative, quiet, literal, realistic, and practical. They are careful, precise, logical, honest, and matter of fact. They tend to be resistant to change and comfortable with routines, are hard working, and responsible. The most important thing to ISTJs is being of service, working hard, and being responsible.

ISTJs are dependable pillars of strength. They often try to reform other people. They tend to make good bank examiners, auditors, accountants, tax examiners, supervisors in libraries, hospitals, and businesses, as well as home economics and physical education teachers.

ISTP

Introverted Sensing Thinking Perceptive "The Mechanics" or "The Crafters"	
Enjoys activity	Reflective
Productive	Factual
Efficient	Sensible
Curious	Practical
Mechanically adept	Rational
Enjoys independence and solitude	Generous

ISTPs tend to be logical, pragmatic, matter of fact, quiet, unassuming, and autonomous. They can be realistic, aloof, impulsive and curious about the physical world. ISTPs are flexible, resourceful, objective, and unemotional.

The most important thing to ISTPs is the freedom to act independently and follow their impulses.

ISTPs are action oriented, fearless, and crave excitement. They are impulsive and dangerous to stop. They often like tools, instruments, weapons, and often become technical experts.

PART III
Unlocking What You Love

Tell me and I'll forget; show me and I may remember;
involve me and I'll understand. - Chinese Proverb

Discovering your personality is the first step in answering the "Who am I?" question. It provides a great deal of insight into the way you take in information, process that information, and solve problems. Understanding this about yourself will help you pinpoint the type of work that will most satisfy you.

In this section you will use your personality information to do some critical thinking and research to discover the answer to the second question, "What should I do with my life?"

CHAPTER 6
Who Are You?

In this exercise, you will need your personality profile from the previous section as well as from some of the *Tools and Resources* mentioned in Part 5. You need to have a full description of your personality type to receive the most benefit from this exercise.

Exercise 1

1. From your personality description in the previous section, list three characteristics that you feel describes you best.

   a) Analytical   b) Visionary

   c) Intellectual

2. From a full description of your personality type, find a brief statement containing an action you feel describes

you well. The action described should be something you enjoy doing. **Ex:** *helping others through my ideas.*

---

3. Use one of the titles provided at the beginning of your personality description in Chapter 5, if you feel it describes you well. If not, create a similar type of title that does describe you. List it below.

---

4. Now, complete the following **personality statement** with your answers from questions 1, 2, and 3.

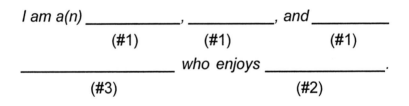

I am a(n) _____, _____, *and* _____
                (#1)   (#1)   (#1)
_____ *who enjoys* _____.
           (#3)   (#2)

An example of this completed statement could be: *I am an* ***articulate, committed, empathetic activist*** *who enjoys* ***being of service to others.***

Wrap Up

Congratulations! You now have a concise, succinct statement that will help you evaluate possible career paths and lines of work. Write this statement down in the *Putting It All Together* section in Chapter 10. You will want to refer to this powerful statement often.

CHAPTER 7

Your skills

Consider some of the things you are good at doing, the skills that seem to come naturally to you or those you have worked to create. For instance, are you good at drawing conclusions, completing math problems, researching information, writing, helping others solve their problems, fixing things, making things, working with children, working with the elderly, or working with animals?

Everyone has a unique set of skills, talents, and gifts. Knowledge of these, combined with knowledge about your personality, provides you with a wealth of information to help you answer the question, "What should I do with my life?"

Take some time to brainstorm, creating a list of the skills you possess. Consider both the natural skills that have always come easy to you as well as those you have developed through education and work experiences. Do not discount any skill at this point, even if you think it is not the type of skill you could use "on the job." This list of your skills will help you further identify the types of work you would enjoy and at which you would excel. Give this list some thought and take your time. If you are having difficulty brainstorming about this list, ask your parents or other trusted family members, friends, or teachers for ideas about what they think you do well. Sometimes another's perspective will help with such an exercise. Keep in mind though, that this is *your* list, and it must ring true for you.

Exercise 2

Natural skills

_____

_____

_____

_____

_____

_____

Developed skills

_____

_____

_____

_____

_____

_____

Now, choose five skills that you feel are your best skills from either category and list them below.

1) _____

2) _____

3) _____

4) _____

5) _____

Wrap Up

Add your five top skills to the *Putting It All Together* section in Chapter 10.

This is your second powerful key, one that will help you unlock the myriad of career choices that are available and will help you find work you will love.

CHAPTER 8

Your personality needs

Your personality profile has provided you valuable keys to unlock your identity and your unique character traits. For you to live in harmony with your personality, your very identity, your personality needs should also be met. By finding work that not only makes use of your personal character traits, but also satisfies the needs of your personality, you will be able to identify the type of work you will love.

Since no one job can satisfy all of the needs of your personality, you should prioritize the top needs that will ensure your happiness in a chosen line of work. Keep in mind that those personality needs that are not fulfilled at work can be satisfied through your hobbies and other interests.

Return to a full description of your personality type and start to identify some of your personality needs. In the descriptions of your personality type, look for descriptions of ways you *need* to express yourself, or how you *need* to process information, or how you *need* to interact with others. Even though your personality description may not use the word "need" per se, you will know you have found a personality need if you find it repeated in several of your personality descriptions, or if the description states that this quality is of great importance to your personality type.

Exercise 3

In the chart that follows, rank your top five personality needs in order of importance to you. Place your most important need in the number one position and work down from there.

Some examples of personality needs could be:

- To help others reach their potential
- Able to make decisions and act on them

Ranking	Personality Need
1	
2	
3	
4	
5	

Wrap Up

Through this ranking exercise, you now have a prioritized list of five of your personality needs that you would like to meet through your chosen line of work. When you begin to think of jobs and careers, you can now evaluate whether a position will allow you to satisfy these needs. This is powerful information to have, since many people do not even know why they hate their job so much. Most often, it is because the job they have does not meet their top five personality needs.

Add this ranking to its proper place in the *Putting It All Together* section in Chapter 10. You are almost there. Only one more set of exercises to go! This is a good point to take a break and come back to the last exercise with a rested mind.

CHAPTER 9

Career suggestions

Many of the personality profiles you have been reading provided possible career suggestions for each personality type. Some of them might have interested you, while others did not. It is time to discover why some of those suggestions were made for your personality type and how they might match your skills and needs. Remember, understanding why some careers interest you and why others do not will enable you to find work you love.

Exercise 4

1. Research some of the career possibilities for your personality type from some of the resources suggested in Part 5. From the numerous suggestions, choose three that most interest you and one about which you are unsure, but would like to know more.

Careers that seem interesting:

a) _____

b) _____

c) _____

Career I would like to know more about:

d) _____

2. Use some career sites like *www.jobprofiles.org*, the Federal Occupational Outlook Handbook located online at *http://stats.bls.gov/oco/ocoiab.htm#A* or job sites like *www.monster.com* to do some research on each career. Try to find out what people with those careers do each day, what they enjoy about that career, and what challenges exist in the field. The more information you are able to find about each career, the more helpful this exercise will be.

What do these four careers seem to have in common?

To answer this question, it is very helpful to use a Venn diagram to compare and contrast the characteristics of the careers you have researched. A Venn diagram is a logical way to graphically organize a large amount of complex information so that you can readily discover areas of commonality and make connections between seemingly disparate items. Venn diagrams were invented by the nineteenth-century mathematician John Venn. They can easily be used as a way to visualize relationships between two or more items.[19]

Venn diagrams have traditionally been used to evaluate premises in logic and probability mathematics. They have also been used in educational settings to compare and contrast elements of literature, scientific concepts, as well as a self-discovery tool – the way you will use a Venn diagram here.

Use the Venn diagrams that follow to organize the information resulting from your research. To use the Venn diagrams, place characteristics that are common to both careers in the center section and characteristics that are unique to each career on either side. An example of a completed Venn diagram follows.

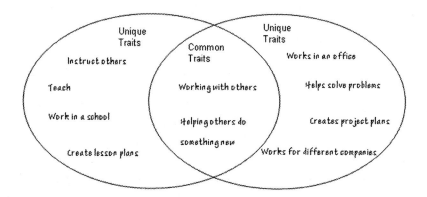

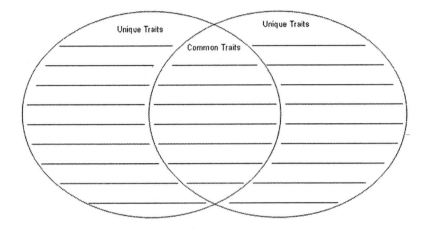

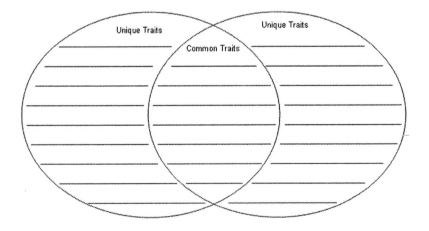

3. Record the common career traits you listed in the center of each Venn diagram.

_____

_____

_____

_____

_____

_____

_____

4. Consider the common career traits you just listed in step 3. (A) Choose three traits that you would most like to use and list them on the left of the chart that follows. (B) How do these common career traits fit your personality? Find out by matching each career trait with one of your personality traits from Exercise 1 (or other traits you may not have listed) on the right column of the chart.

Career trait (A)	Personality trait (B)

Record the three career traits you just listed in column A in its proper place in the *Putting It All Together* section in Chapter 10.

5. Go back to step 1 of this exercise. Consider the four careers you chose to explore. Brainstorm and create a list of the skills these four careers would require.

_____

_____

_____

_____

_____

_____

_____

_____

6. Are any of the skills you listed in step 5 similar to those you listed previously as your strengths in Chapter 7? Determine to what degree you possess the skills you listed in the previous steps of this exercise. In the following table write down several of the skills you listed in the previous step. Then, on a scale of one to four, rate your strength in each skill.

Skills used in the careers you are exploring	Rate your strength in this skill. (1) Need to develop (4) Very strong
Example: Verbal and written communication	1 2 (3) 4
	1 2 3 4
	1 2 3 4
	1 2 3 4

Skills used in the careers you are exploring	Rate your strength in this skill. (1) Need to develop (4) Very strong		
	1 2 3 4		
	1 2 3 4		
	1 2 3 4		
	1 2 3 4		

Wrap Up

This was an intense exercise and you covered a lot of ground. Congratulations! Based on this exercise, you now have an understanding of the common career traits that your personality type enjoys expressing through work. You have identified which of those traits match your own personality traits. Additionally, you have discovered the skills some of those careers require and your strength in those skills. By putting all the information you have learned together, you can now continue on to find the work you love.

On the next page, take the time to complete any unfinished section in your one page guide in Chapter 10. Once it is complete, you may want to photocopy your one page guide as you work to identify and pursue work you love.

CHAPTER 10
Putting it all together

You have just completed a great deal of research and critical thinking about yourself, your personality, and the characteristics you possess and wish to express in a chosen line of work. Now, it is time to finish putting all of this together in a concise, one page summary that you can use to find work you will love.

My One-Page Guide to Finding Work I Will Love

Who am I?

(Personality statement from Exercise 1, Step 4)

I am a _____, _____, and _____
_____ who enjoys _____.

What should I do with my life?

In order to answer this question I will need to look for work that will...

(Your 5 best skills from Exercise 2)
Use my best skills including:

* _____
* _____
* _____
* _____
* _____

(Your top 5 personality needs from Exercise 3)
Satisfy my personality needs that include:

1. _____
2. _____
3. _____
4. _____
5. _____

(Career list from Exercise 4, Step 4)
Allow me to:

* _____
* _____
* _____

(Career suggestions from Exercise 4, Step 1)
Possible lines of work I will love include, but are not limited to:

_____   _____   _____

PART VI
Now What?

Every moment in planning saves 3 or 4 in execution.
- Crawford Greenwalt
Just don't give up what you're trying to do. Where there is
love and inspiration, I don't think you can go wrong.
- Ella Fitzgerald

Your *One Page Guide to Finding Work You Love* will help you think outside the box as you search for work you love. Searching job boards can often be discouraging when you keep running across positions that feel limiting or uninteresting. Quite often, the positions that could be customized to your particular strengths and personality needs are not advertised. They barely even exist within an organization. For instance, a department within a company may be overloaded with work and may not be functioning efficiently. However, the company does not necessarily recognize that they need to hire someone with your unique skills and personality traits. Therefore, you need to take the initiative to become a problem-solver and start to look for situations and circumstances where you would shine. Since you have done the work to identify the exact type of position that you would love, you can help the potential hiring manager solve his or her problem in their department, while in the process creating the very work you will love.

This tactic requires research into industries and companies that match your personality needs and traits. Granted, this requires a more active role than the average job seeker takes, but then the rewards are also greater when you create that perfect match.

Think this tactic would fail in the real world? Think again. I have successfully used this tactic more than once.

In one instance, I helped create a new position within a company where I was already working at the time. This was when I was working for the tour company in Washington, D.C. I had begun to tire of giving tours and needed to use more of my skills and have other personality needs met. By working closely with the general manager, I learned that the company wanted to expand its business into tours for students. Since I had been a middle school teacher, I was asked if I would be interested in working on such a project. I jumped at the opportunity, since I knew that problem solving, creating new things, and managing projects were tasks that I did well, but I did not have the opportunity to use them in my current function within the company. In this instance, understanding my own personality had the benefit of allowing me to seize the opportunities that were available.

The second time I used this tactic was to move to a new company. At this time, I had nearly completed my work on my MBA and was looking for work in project management at a rapidly growing medium to large company. Through research I had conducted for an MBA project, I was able to identify a few companies that interested me. I began to think about what problems individual departments at those companies might need to solve and how I could assist in solving them. Several months later, I met with a hiring manager and we discussed the issues his department was having. I accepted a position with that department and that led to other opportunities within that same company.

By having a clear understanding not only of your skills and strengths, but also of your personality traits and your work preferences, you can redesign your resume and tailor your job search to focus on the types of positions that will bring you fulfillment. Finally, you will be able to find work you love. There is no magic wand to instantly create the position you will love, but the understanding you now have will allow you to focus on the areas you wish to utilize in your next position or career.

CHAPTER 11
Next Steps

The following are subsequent steps you can take to build on what you have learned about yourself and find the work you will love.

- **Continue to research career possibilities.** The work you have done in this book was just the beginning. The exploration into careers is something not given enough time during high school and college. Internships, opportunities to "shadow" someone in your chosen career, and informational interviews are all great ways to gather real information about the types of jobs you are considering. (In an informational interview, you are not asking for a job, but are asking for time with someone in a career that interests you, to ask questions about that career. Please see *Tools and Resources* for more information on information interviews.)

- **Redraft your resume to highlight your top skills and personality strengths.** This will cast you in the best light in front of potential employers. When you interview, you will be able to speak with confidence about these top skills and strengths. For information on resume writing, see the *Tools and Resources* section.

- **Determine if additional training, schooling, or certification will give you an edge in the line of work you would like to pursue.** Higher education needs to serve as a means to an end, and not as a goal in itself. An undergraduate degree will open many doors that would be closed to those without such a degree. However, since an undergraduate college education has become a reality for many individuals, you will need to think of ways to stand out from the crowd. This can often be accomplished with a certificate in your chosen field or even a graduate degree. Consider all options when looking at additional education, such as accredited online and distance education programs. Many such programs recognize the time constraints on working adults and offer flexible class schedules and payment options.

- **Stay current on developments in the field you are pursuing.** Determine what professional organizations and trade journals or magazines are important to those in your chosen field. In order to be a problem-solver for your potential employer, you need to be familiar with the issues in the field.

- **Share your search with others.** As you focus on finding work you love, begin to share that information with others who can help you. In a word, network. You will be able to multiply your own efforts by letting others know exactly what you are looking for. You will find additional sources about networking in the *Tools and Resources* section.

- **Work with a coach.** Just as Tiger Woods has a coach to help him improve his game and maintain focus, you can too. Focusing yourself and finding work you love is hard work. It is often easy to get discouraged and not see beyond your own blind spots. These are the very things a career coach can help you to do.

> *Twenty years from now you will be more disappointed by the things you didn't do than by the ones you did do. So throw off the bowlines. Sail away from the safe harbor. Catch the trade winds in your sails. Explore. Dream. Discover. - Mark Twain*

PART VII
Tools and Resources

If my mind can conceive it, and my heart can believe it,
I know I can achieve it. -Jesse Jackson

Personality Type

Humanmetrics Jung Typology Test:
http://www.humanmetrics.com/cgi-win/JTypes1.htm
This free test provides a very good indication of your personality type. Includes 72 questions that, when scored, will deliver your four-letter code and a rather detailed description.

What is Your Personality Type?:
http://www.personalitytype.com/quiz.asp
This site features a very simple quiz created by Barbara Barron-Tieger and Paul Tieger, authors of *Do What You Are*. It quickly provides your four-letter personality code

along with a brief description of your type and possible career possibilities.

Personality Descriptions and Career Possibilities by Wayne State College in Nebraska:
http://www.wsc.edu/advising/program/career/personality/
> This site provides a very detailed description of the 16 personality types along with several career suggestions for each type.

Personality and Career Tests:
http://jobsearch.about.com/library/weekly/aa011803b.htm
> Provides information and links to several personality assessments including the MBTI, the Keirsey Temperament Sorter, and the Strong Interest Inventory. Fee involved.

Motivational Appraisal of Personal Potential:
http://www.assessment.com/
> MAPP is a fully integrated, computer-aided vocational assessment system capable of matching people with jobs. Free registration required and access to test sent to email address provided. Very detailed sample results are provided free of charge. Complete results can be obtained starting at $19.95.

A Modern Guide to the Four Temperaments by Stephen Montgomery, PhD:
http://keirsey.com/matrix.html

> This site describes the 16 personality types divided into four categories, called temperaments.

Erikson's Development Theory

Erikson, Erik. *Childhood and Society*. New York, NY: W.W. Norton and Company, 1963.

> This book is the original source in which Erikson explains his theory of human development.

http://www.childdevelopmentinfo.com/development/erickson.shtml

> The site, maintained by the Child Development Institute, provides an overview of the eight stages of development.

Erikson's Development Stages. Patient Teaching, Loose Leaf Library. Springhouse Corporation (1990).
http://honolulu.hawaii.edu/intranet/committees/FacDevCom/guidebk/teachtip/erikson.htm

> This site, maintained by Honolulu Community College, provides a brief description of all eight of Erikson's development stages.

Schultz D.P. and Schultz S.E. *A History of Modern Psychology*. Orlando, FL: Harcourt-Brace.

> This text provides a clear, well-organized, user-friendly overview of modern psychology, presenting the evolution of the schools of thought as a continuing story.

> An online version adapted from this text can be found at http://web.cortland.edu/andersmd/ERIK/stageint.HTML

Information Interviews and Networking

"Informational Interviewing: Get the Inside Scoop on Careers":

http://www.bls.gov/opub/ooq/2002/summer/art03.pdf

> Excellent article from the U.S. Department of Labor, Bureau of Labor Statistics - Occupational Outlook Quarterly, 2002

Informational Interviewing Tutorial by Quintessential Careers:

http://www.quintcareers.com/informational_interviewing.html

> This site provides a good overview of the information interview.

Information Interview:

http://www.career.fsu.edu/ccis/guides/infoint.html

This site, maintained by The Career Center at Florida State University, defines an information interview and provides guidance on how to set up and prepare for an information interview.

Information Interview:
http://danenet.wicip.org/jets/jet-9407-p.html
This site provides a brief overview of the information interview and 20 sample questions to use.

Networking:
http://careers.utah.edu/cs/jobsearch/networkingtips.htm
This site, maintained by Career Services at University of Utah, provides tips on how to network and incorporates the use of the information interview.

Resume Writing

http://www.rockportinstitute.com/resumes.html
A six-part article from the Rockport Institute describes how to write a master resume.

http://resume.monster.com/
This site provides resume services and tips from Monster.com.

Endnotes

[1] Alexandra Robbins and Abbey Wilner, *Quarterlife Crisis: the Unique Challenges of Life in Your Twenties,* (New York: Penguin Putnam, 2001), p. 7.

[2] Ibid, p. 38.

[3] *The Psychology Dictionary.* All Psych Online from http:// allpsych.com/dictionary.

[4] Merovingian in The Matrix Reloaded, Warner Video (2003)

[5] Ibid.

[6] D.P. Schultz and S.E. Schultz. *A History of Modern Psychology.* (Orlando, FL: Harcourt-Brace, 1987)

[7] Erikson, Erik,*Childhood and Society*, (New York, NY: W.W. Norton and Company, 1963), p. 247.

[8] Ibid. p. 251.

[9] Ibid. p. 255.

[10] Ibid. p. 258.

[11] Ibid. p. 261.

[12] Ibid.

[13] Rachel Osterman, "Old Room, New Rules: Grads Move Back in With Mom, Dad", *Chicago Tribune*, August 23, 2004, p. 1.

[14] Erik Erikson, *Identity Youth and Crisis,* (New York, NY: W.W. Norton and Company, 1968), p.128.

[15] C. George Boeree, PhD. *Current Topics in Psychology.* Available at www.fenichel.com

[16] Ibid.

[17] Carl Jung,. *Portable Jung.* (New York: Penguin Books, 1971).

[18] Ibid.

[19] Dennis Rohatyn, *Logic.* (Blacklick, OH: McGraw-Hill Professional Book Group, 1998). p. 116. http://site. ebrary.com/lib/cecybrary/Doc?id=5004534&page=123

Printed in the United States
28370LVS00001B/139